Real love stories

NEVER HAVE ENDINGS.

RICHARD BACH

TO

_____

FROM

_____

In Case I Haven't
Told You
I love you because...

KIMBERLY SHUMATE

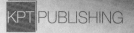

IN ALL THE WORLD there is but one constant and resounding timpani that beats out the rhythm of spectacular love—that is the human heart. Extraordinary romance can be found in ordinary places…

the cool trickle of rainfall

a garden drenched in perfume

a hand gently cradled in another.

In case I haven't told you, I love you because…

YOU INSPIRE ME

to dream.

ABOUT THE AUTHOR

Kimberly is a freelance writer, and is profoundly moved by the depth in which a human heart can feel. Her poetic prose and sentimental view of life and love bring radiant hues to a canvas that can too often lose its luster.

"There is nothing about the art of love that is mundane—
it is sublime in every shade, contour, and frame."

I love you because...
TIME IS ON OUR SIDE

I said only one word,

brought only one message:

Love.

Love and nothing else.

NIKOS KAZANTZAKIS

Call the second hand

down from the wall.

Stop the hourglass

sands to fall.

FREEZE THE WAVES UPON THE SHORE,

AND PREVENT THE WINDS

FROM CREATING MORE.

REMOVE THE MOUNTAINS AND EMPTY THE SEA;

TAKE ALL THAT YOU ARE

OR WILL EVER BE.

Lovers need to know
how to lose themselves
and then
how to find themselves again.

PAULO COELHO

Erase the rush of rivers flow,
delete the answers to all we know.

Until what is left

becomes what is right;

to all we call dear,

EMBELLISHED AND BRIGHT.

Hold what's in motion perfectly still;

do with the future whatever you will.

For there is nothing on earth

that can frighten me now,

FOR YOU HAVE RENEWED ME

WITH ONE SINGLE VOW.

If I had a flower

for every time I thought of you,

I could walk

through my garden forever.

ALFRED LORD TENNYSON

True love is
eternal, infinite,
and always like itself,
it is equal and pure...
it is seen with white hairs
and is always young in heart.

HONORÉ DE BALZAC

I LOVE YOU MORE IN THIS MOMENT

THAN A LIFETIME COULD HOLD.

KEEP CLOSE, MY BELOVED,

STAY HERE AND BE BOLD.

MAY TIME BE KIND

AND FORGIVE NOW AND THEN.

MAY THE DAYS, MONTHS,

AND YEARS REMAIN

OUR FAITHFUL TRUE FRIEND.

Love has no age,

no limit;

and no death.

JOHN GALSWORTHY

Love consists in this:

that two solitudes

protect and touch

and greet each other.

RAINER MARIA RILKE

I Love You Because...

Your Hand

Fits *Perfectly*

in Mine

OUR TWO HANDS
FOLD CONTENTLY INTO ONE.
Whether cradled fingers
hide beneath the coat sleeves
of a crystal white winter,
or entwine in the open air
of spring's colorful splendor,
our lasting bond
WILL ENDURE FOREVER.

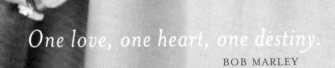

One love, one heart, one destiny.

BOB MARLEY

Hidden in gentle shelter,
each soft, quiet curve blends to its mate.
Our hands remain faithful
to hold tightly together
while other hands are quick to let go,
pushing love away.

Love is composed of
a single soul
inhabiting two bodies.

ARISTOTLE

Whatever treasures unearthed

or hand may find in store—

a ruby in the sand,

a diamond in a promise,

a pearl on the ocean's floor—

my hand found the richest reward

when it found its way to yours.

Where there is the greatest love,
there are always miracles.

WILLA CATHER

When you love someone,
you love the person
as they are,
and not as
you'd like them to be.

LEO TOLSTOY

I Love You Because…

Loving You Is Easy

*I've seldom allowed myself
to bend beneath the weight
of romantic risk.
It was better to resist love
than to reveal
my fragile heart.*

Love takes off masks

that we fear we cannot live without

and know

we cannot live with.

I would never think
to show my tears
when pressures mounted
and troubles neared.

To act shaken
might convince
dilemmas to appear.

So I hid from difficulties,
from love, from life.

I tried yet failed
for they would not
push aside.

THE MOMENT YOU HAVE IN YOUR HEART
this extraordinary thing called love
and feel the depth,
the delight,
the ecstasy of it,
YOU WILL DISCOVER
that for you
the world is transformed.

JIDDU KRISHNAMURTI

Then your loving spirit
touched me
with profound effect.
All at once I came to know
what every lover should in time.

Love is when
you meet someone
who tells you
something new
about yourself.

ANDRE BRETON

IT'S BETTER TO BELIEVE THAT LOVE WILL WIN,

that it will somehow find a way.

That its power can restore a life

that might have gone astray.

TO WALK THE PATH TOGETHER,

in the center of Destiny's plan.

And with each step you've taught me

how to heal and love again.

In you, I see forever—
see how we are together.
You have slowly exposed
    a strange and marvelous view.
Yes, it's never been so easy
to be in love with you.

The face is the mirror
of the mind,
and eyes without speaking
confess the secrets
of the heart.

ST. JEROME

Love is like playing the piano.

First you must learn to play by the rules,

then you must forget the rules

and play from your heart.

Have a heart that never hardens,
and a temper that never tires,
and a touch that never hurts.

CHARLES DICKENS

And as I cling to my champion,
my partner in life,
I've learned that
        it is the heart
        that mends all.
From your eyes I see
        heaven's view from above.
    Continue, my darling,
        to lead with your love.

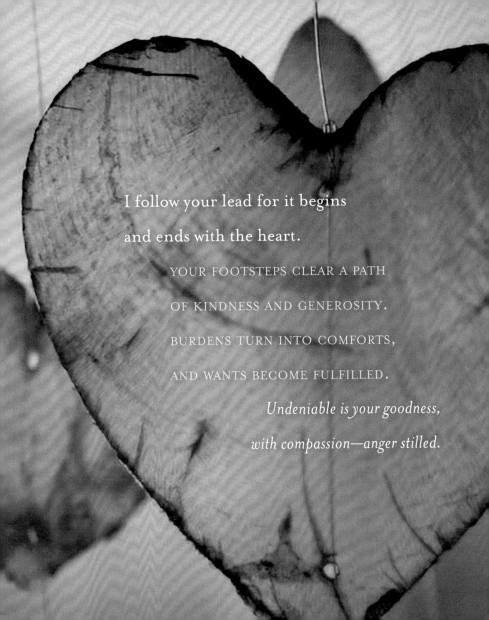

I follow your lead for it begins

and ends with the heart.

YOUR FOOTSTEPS CLEAR A PATH

OF KINDNESS AND GENEROSITY.

BURDENS TURN INTO COMFORTS,

AND WANTS BECOME FULFILLED.

Undeniable is your goodness,

with compassion—anger stilled.

FAITH

makes all things possible...

LOVE

makes all things easy.

DWIGHT L. MOODY

What amiable arms hold me?
What insight you've shown me.
Every stranger is a friend,
every trial about to end.

Love possesses not
nor will it be possessed,
for love is sufficient
unto love.

KHALIL GIBRAN

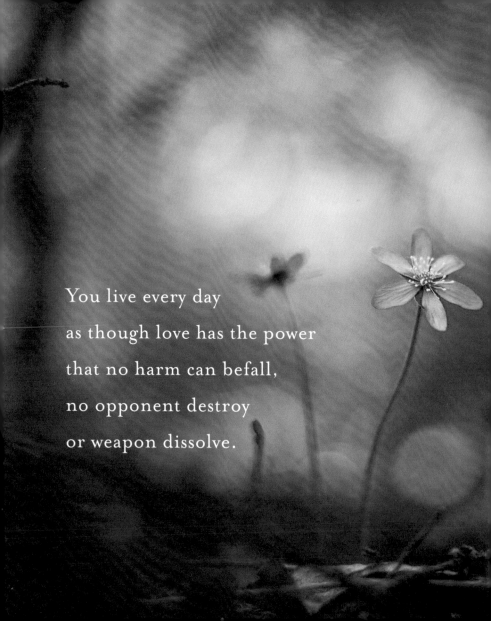

You live every day
as though love has the power
that no harm can befall,
no opponent destroy
or weapon dissolve.

You can give without loving,

but you can never love without giving.

ROBERT LOUIS STEVENSON

With a hand so gentle,

you help carry my cares

as no one else

has ever dared.

A kind heart

is a fountain of gladness,

making everything

in its vicinity

freshen into smiles.

WASHINGTON IRVING

I Love You Because... *Even the Rain Becomes You*

Liquid pearls dance upon your skin,

with laughter the iridescent drops

trickle down around your chin.

Your damp lips bring refreshment

to mine and in such gentleness,

your kiss bears more passion

than summer's sunshine.

In the sweetness of friendship
let there be laughter
and sharing of pleasures.
For in the dew of little things
the heart finds
its morning and is refreshed.

KHALIL GIBRAN

The gleam of your eyes,

the rainbow necklace

around your neck,

your cheeks drenched with

a shower of broken clouds;

my hand reaches for yours.

And as your touch washes over me,

suddenly the downpour

gives way

to an everlasting sky.

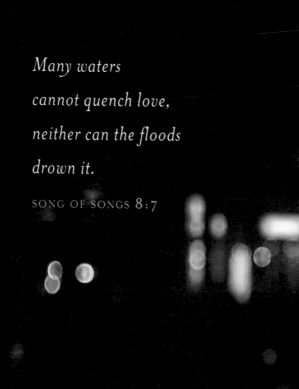

*Many waters
cannot quench love,
neither can the floods
drown it.*

SONG OF SONGS 8:7

Dripping with shimmering light,

you glimmer with the radiance

of a king's ransom.

Every droplet is a gem disguised.

Love is life.

And if you miss love,

you miss life.

LEO BUSCAGLIA

Abandoned vanity,

we dance in the rain

as others retreat from beneath

the restless clouds.

We are changed into children again.

The best thing

to hold onto in life

is each other.

AUDREY HEPBURN

Dear love, Dear life,

while I remain next to you

and as I live

and love you so,

I've realized that

even the rain becomes you.

Love *doesn't* make

the world go 'round.

Love *is* what makes

the ride worthwhile.

FRANKLIN P. JONES

If you love a flower,
don't pick it up...
let it be.
Love is not about possession.
Love is about appreciation.

OSHO

I Love You Because… *You're My Favorite Work of Art*

All things grow old…
the world's finest museums
and all that they hold.
Even the grandest works
of art lose their luster—
marble columns, statues,
busts, and paintings in the Louvre.
Even nature's vibrant buds wither
when their season
of enchantment is through.

Falling in love

consists merely in uncorking

the imagination

and bottling

the common sense.

HELEN ROWLAND

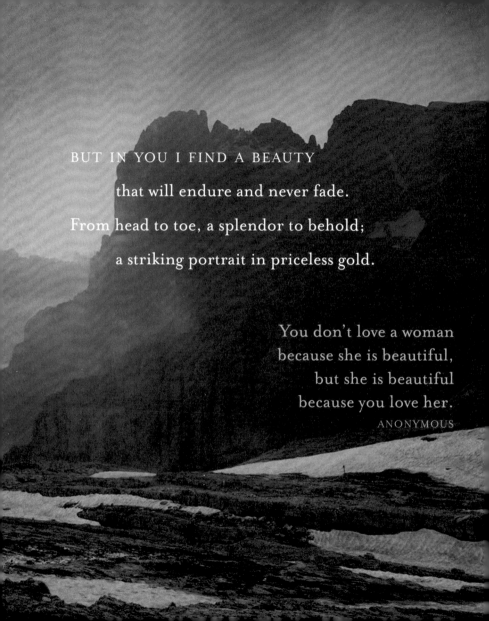

BUT IN YOU I FIND A BEAUTY
that will endure and never fade.
From head to toe, a splendor to behold;
a striking portrait in priceless gold.

You don't love a woman
because she is beautiful,
but she is beautiful
because you love her.
ANONYMOUS

I should like to name

every freckle, line,

and wisp of hair

that a brush stroke of genius

could not compare.

In our life, there is a single color

as on an artist's palette,

which provides the meaning of life and art.

It is the color of love.

MARC CHAGALL

As the Mona Liza smiles

shyly into the crowd,

I see you beside me,

the most precious possession

any gallery could endow.

In my mind,

let me frame every breath,

every look…

enthralling illustrations

in our splendid

co-authored book.

Of all the music that reached

farthest into heaven,

it is the beating of a loving heart.

HENRY WARD BEECHER

Your smile
makes music
where once
there was none.
Your heart
beholds only
what love
can become.

We don't love someone for their looks,

or their clothes,

or for their fancy car,

but because they sing a song

only you can hear.

OSCAR WILDE

WITHIN THE MULTITUDE OF EARTHLY VAULTS,
sublime creations by hands rich with faults;
the art of mere humans
celebrated great and small—
take heart.
Dear One, you above all these
are my favorite work of art.

Trust your heart if the seas catch fire,
live by love
though the stars walk backward.

E. E. CUMMINGS

The day that man allows true love to appear,
those things which are well made
will fall into confusion
and will overturn everything
we believe to be right and true.

DANTE ALIGHIERI

I love you because...

You Never Cease to Surprise Me

You know me so well and,
at times, take advantage of my predictableness.
How you tickle and entertain me
with all you possess.
Surely, no one else has such a gift
as rare and completely fabulous!

We waste time looking for the perfect love,

instead of creating the perfect love.

TOM ROBBINS

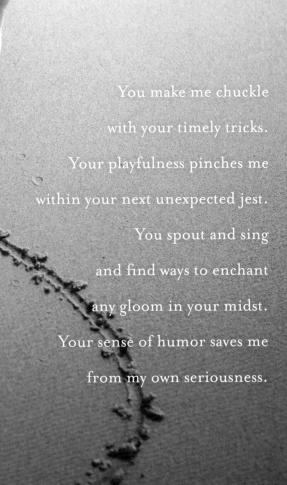

You make me chuckle

with your timely tricks.

Your playfulness pinches me

within your next unexpected jest.

You spout and sing

and find ways to enchant

any gloom in your midst.

Your sense of humor saves me

from my own seriousness.

LOVE RECOGNIZES NO BARRIERS.

It jumps hurdles, leaps fences,

penetrates walls to arrive

at its destination full of hope.

MAYA ANGELOU

A true friend
is someone
who lets you
have total freedom
to be yourself.

JIM MORRISON

You are good for me—
to laugh and pretend and utterly adore love.
To tease and quip
and hoax and prank.
Childlike banter
to ease life's anxious delays.

So, my Love, lift your eyes
     to see all the ways
     you unwrap my disguise.
In truth, there's no end
     to your methods
     to delight and surprise.

Love has nothing to do with

what you are expecting to get,

only with what you are expecting to give,

which is everything.

So, I love you because...

the entire universe

conspired to help me

find you.

PAULO COELHO

In Case I Haven't Told You

© 2018 KPT Publishing, LLC
Written by Kimberly Shumate

Published by KPT Publishing
Minneapolis, Minnesota 55406
www.KPTPublishing.com

ISBN 978-1-944833-54-1

Designed by AbelerDesign.com

First printing January 2019

10 9 8 7 6 5 4 3 2 1

Printed in the United States of America